The Chronnoisseur

Flower Journal

The Chronnoisseur by Justin Klein

www.lulu.com

Cover Design: Todd M. Schilling Design
Interior Design: Todd M. Schilling Design
Editor: Justin Klein
ISBN: 978-1-329-99717-2

The purpose of this journal is to chronicle the consumption of cannabis for individuals who like to enjoy the different flavors, aromas, and methods of consumption available. I hope this book will encourage people to savor the variation between different strains as well as the variations between the same strains from different growers and regions. This journal will be a means for you to note the flavors, appearance, method of consumption, as well as the overall experience you like the best and least. Utilize this as a quick reference guide to determine whether you would like a future choice in product, and whether that product has unbeknownst to you already been consumed by you in the method of which you are currently about to try again; because, let's be honest, sometimes we forget.

Enjoy Responsibly!

How to Fill Out

In the dispensary section list the name and/or location from which you purchased your cannabis. This will allow you to differentiate between strains in different regions and from dispensary/growers in the same region. The date section can be used as a reference to see whether the characteristics of your cannabis, or even your palate, have changed over time.

Next it is important to list the strain name of the cannabis you are tasting. Check whether the strain is an indica, sativa, or both for hybrid. The $/g section is meant for you to note the difference in prices between regions, dispensaries, and strains.

The next few sections are meant to help in describing the cannabis prior to consumption. Utilize the blank bars and pie charts under each heading to shade in the level of each descriptor written. The blank description area of this section should be used to elaborate on everything that the shading can not fully express.

These next sections will be used to describe the consumption of the cannabis. Under the method section, circle whether you consumed the cannabis through a joint, waterpipe or dry pipe. Fill out the taste and smoke sections in the same manner as you did with the shading above. The blank description under this section should be utilized to elaborate on the type of method of consumption, as well as the characteristics of the taste and smoke.

The final section is to capture your overall impression of the cannabis strain. Rate your overall experience on a scale of 1 through 10 and circle yes or no depending on whether you would recommend this strain to a peer. Under experience you can describe what type of affect the cannabis had on you and a story of something that may have occurred while under the influence of that particular strain, using that particular method.

The following page is an example of how to complete the pages of your journal.

Date **7/15**

Dispensary (name/location)   **XYZ Naturals - MT**

Strain   **Silvertip**   indica ☑ Price   **10** $/g
sativa ☑

Color   Crystal   Density   Scent

Large ☐ Heavy   Rock ☐ Tight   Heavy ☐

Small ☐ Light   Loose ☐ Airy   Light ☐

Size / Coverage

Pine/Earthy   Citrus   Skunk/Cheese   Floral

Description   **Semi-dense bud, easy to break up, lots of crystals,**
Full bodied scent with dominate notes of skunk and floral

Taste   Smoke

Floral Citrus   Heavy ☐ Full

Fruity / Cheese

Peppery / Nutty   Light ☐ Whispy

Spicy Earthy

Description   **Smoked out of blue sherlock named "Petey"**
heavier smoke, with dominate earthy/florally flavor

Overall   **8** /10   Recommend   (Yes) No

Experience   **very heady/relaxing high, great for nausea, movies,**
passenger on road trips, and blowing smoke rings

Date _____

Dispensary (name/location) _____

Strain _____   indica ☐   Price _____ $/g
                                sativa ☐

Color
Green Yellow
Blue   Orange
Violet Red

Crystal
Large ☐ ☐ Heavy
Small ☐ ☐ Light
Size Coverage

Density
Rock ☐ Tight
Loose ☐ Airy

Scent
Heavy ☐ ☐ ☐ ☐
Light ☐ ☐ ☐ ☐
Pine/Earthy Citrus Skunk/Cheese Floral

Description _____
_____

Taste
Floral Citrus
Fruity   Cheese
Peppery   Nutty
Spicy Earthy

Smoke
Heavy ☐ Full
Light ☐ Whispy

Description _____
_____

Overall _____ /10   Recommend   Yes / No

Experience _____
_____
_____

Date _____

_____

Strain _____

indica ☐
sativa ☐

Price _____ $/g

Color

Green Yellow

Orange

Violet Red

Crystal

Large ☐ ☐ Heavy

Small ☐ ☐ Light

Size Coverage

Density

Rock ☐ Tight

Loose ☐ Airy

Scent

Heavy ☐ ☐ ☐ ☐

Light

Pine/Earthy Citrus Skunk/Cheese Floral

Description _____

_____

Taste

Floral Citrus

Fruity Cheese

Peppery Nutty

Spicy Earthy

Smoke

Heavy ☐ Full

Light ☐ Whispy

Description _____

_____

Overall _____ /10

Recommend   Yes / No

Experience _____

_____

_____

Date _____

Dispensary (name/location) _____

Strain _____
indica ☐
sativa ☐

Price _____ $/

Color

Green Yellow
Blue   Orange
Violet Red

Crystal

Large ☐ ☐ Heavy
Small ☐ ☐ Light
Size Coverage

Density

Rock ☐ Tight
Loose ☐ Airy

Scent

Heavy ☐ ☐ ☐
Light ☐ ☐ ☐
Pine/Earthy Citrus Skunk/Cheese Floral

Description _____

Taste

Floral Citrus
Fruity   Cheese
Peppery   Nutty
Spicy Earthy

Smoke

Heavy ☐ Full
Light ☐ Whisp.

Description _____

Overall _____ /10

Recommend _____ Yes / No

Experience _____

Date _____

Dispensary (name/location) _____

Strain _____ indica ☐ Price _____ $/g
                            sativa ☐

Color

Green Yellow
Blue   Orange
Violet Red

Crystal

Large ☐ ☐ Heavy
Small ☐ ☐ Light

Size *Coverage*

Density

Rock ☐ Tight
Loose ☐ Airy

Scent

Heavy ☐ ☐ ☐ ☐
Light ☐

Pine/Earthy *Citrus* *Skunk/Cheese* *Floral*

Description _____

_____

Taste

Floral Citrus
Fruity   Cheese
Peppery   Nutty
Spicy Earthy

Smoke

Heavy ☐ Full
Light ☐ Whispy

Description _____

_____

Overall _____ /10 _____   Recommend Yes / No

Experience _____

_____

_____

Date _____

Dispensary (name/location) _____

Strain _____

indica ☐
sativa ☐

Price _____ $/g

Color

Green Yellow
Blue Orange
Violet Red

Crystal

Large ☐ ☐ Heavy
Small ☐ ☐ Light

Size

Coverage

Density

Rock ☐ Tight
Loose ☐ Airy

Scent

Heavy ☐ ☐ ☐ ☐
Light ☐

Pine/Earthy

Citrus

Skunk/Cheese

Floral

Description _____

Taste

Floral Citrus
Fruity Cheese
Peppery Nutty
Spicy Earthy

Smoke

Heavy ☐ Full
Light ☐ Whispy

Description _____

Overall _____ /10

Recommend Yes / No

Experience _____

Date _____

Dispensary (name/location) _____

Strain _____ indica ☐ Price _____ $/g
                        sativa ☐

Color

Green Yellow
Orange
Violet Red

Crystal

Large ☐ ☐ Heavy
Small ☐ ☐ Light
Size Coverage

Density

Rock ☐ Tight
Loose ☐ Airy

Scent

Heavy ☐ ☐ ☐ ☐ Light
Pine/Earthy Citrus Skunk/Cheese Floral

Description _____

Taste

Floral Citrus
Fruity Cheese
Peppery Nutty
Spicy Earthy

Smoke

Heavy ☐ Full
Light ☐ Whispy

Description _____
_____

Overall _____ /10 _____   Recommend   Yes / No

Experience _____
_____

Date _____

Dispensary (name/location) _____

Strain _____ indica ☐   Price _____ $/g
                                  sativa ☐

Color

Green Yellow
Blue   Orange
   Violet Red

Crystal

Large ☐ ☐ Heavy
Small ☐ ☐ Light
   Size Coverage

Density

Rock ☐ Tight
Loose ☐ Airy

Scent

Heavy ☐ ☐ ☐ ☐
Light ☐ ☐ ☐ ☐
   Pine/Earthy Citrus Skunk/Cheese Floral

Description _____
_____

Taste

Floral Citrus
Fruity   Cheese
Peppery   Nutty
   Spicy Earthy

Smoke

Heavy ☐ Full
Light ☐ Whispy

Description _____
_____

Overall _____ /10 _____   Recommend   Yes / No

Experience _____
_____
_____

Date _____

Dispensary (name/location) _____

Strain _____ indica ☐ Price _____ $/g
sativa ☐

Color

Green Yellow
        Orange
Violet Red

Crystal

Large ☐ ☐ Heavy
Small ☐ ☐ Light

Size Coverage

Density

Rock ☐ Tight
Loose ☐ Airy

Scent

Heavy ☐ ☐ ☐ ☐
Light

Pine/Earthy Citrus Skunk/Cheese Floral

Description _____

_____

Taste

Floral Citrus
Fruity   Cheese
Peppery   Nutty
  Spicy Earthy

Smoke

Heavy ☐ Full
Light ☐ Whispy

Description _____

_____

Overall _____ /10 _____   Recommend   Yes / No

Experience _____

_____

_____

Dispensary (name/location)

Strain

indica ☐
sativa ☐

Price $/

Color

Green   Yellow
Blue   Orange
Violet   Red

Crystal

Large ☐ ☐ Heavy
Small ☐ ☐ Light
Size *Coverage*

Density

Rock ☐ Tight
Loose ☐ Airy

Scent

Heavy ☐ ☐ ☐ ☐
Light ☐ ☐ ☐
Pine/Earthy *Citrus* *Skunk/Cheese* *Floral*

Description

Taste

Floral Citrus
Fruity   Cheese
Peppery   Nutty
Spicy Earthy

Smoke

Heavy ☐ Full
Light ☐ Whisp.

Description

Overall   /10

Recommend   Yes / No

Experience

Date _____

Dispensary (name/location) _____

Strain _____ indica ☐ Price _____ $/g
                         sativa ☐

Color
Green Yellow
Blue   Orange
Violet Red

Crystal
Large ☐ ☐ Heavy
Small ☐ ☐ Light
Size Coverage

Density
Rock ☐ Tight
Loose ☐ Airy

Scent
Heavy ☐ ☐ ☐ ☐
Light
Pine/Earthy Citrus Skunk/Cheese Floral

Description _____
_____

Taste
Floral Citrus
Fruity   Cheese
Peppery   Nutty
Spicy Earthy

Smoke
Heavy ☐ Full
Light ☐ Whispy

Description _____
_____
_____

Overall _____ /10 _____   Recommend   Yes / No

Experience _____
_____
_____

Date _____

Dispensary (name/location) _____

Strain _____

indica ☐
sativa ☐

Price _____ $/g

Color

Green
Yellow
Blue
Orange
Violet
Red

Crystal

Large | Heavy
Small | Light

Size
Coverage

Density

Rock | Tight
Loose | Airy

Scent

Heavy
Light

Pine/Earthy
Citrus
Skunk/Cheese
Floral

Description

_____
_____

Taste

Floral | Citrus
Fruity | Cheese
Peppery | Nutty
Spicy | Earthy

Smoke

Heavy | Full
Light | Whispy

Description

_____
_____

Overall _____ /10 _____

Recommend   Yes / No

Experience

_____
_____
_____

Date _____

Dispensary (name/location) _____

Strain _____ indica ☐   Price _____ $/g
                                    sativa ☐

Color   Crystal   Density   Scent

Green Yellow   Large ☐ ☐ Heavy   Rock ☐ Tight   Heavy ☐ ☐ ☐ ☐
                 Small ☐ ☐ Light   Loose ☐ Airy   Light ☐ ☐ ☐ ☐
        Orange
                      Size Coverage   Pine/Earthy Citrus Skunk/Cheese Floral
Violet Red

Description _____

_____

                          Taste   Smoke

                  Floral Citrus   Heavy ☐ Full
              Fruity   Cheese
                                        Light ☐ Whispy
              Peppery   Nutty

                 Spicy Earthy

Description _____

_____

Overall _____ /10 _____   Recommend   Yes / No

Experience _____

_____

_____

Date _____

Dispensary (name/location) _____

Strain _____ indica ☐ Price _____ $/g
                         sativa ☐

Color

Green Yellow
Blue   Orange
   Violet Red

Crystal

Large ☐ ☐ Heavy
Small ☐ ☐ Light
  Size Coverage

Density

Rock ☐ Tight
Loose ☐ Airy

Scent

Heavy ☐ ☐ ☐ ☐
Light ☐ ☐ ☐ ☐
  Pine/Earthy Citrus Skunk/Cheese Floral

Description _____
_____

Taste

Floral Citrus
Fruity   Cheese
Peppery   Nutty
   Spicy Earthy

Smoke

Heavy ☐ Full
Light ☐ Whispy

Description _____
_____

Overall _____ /10 _____   Recommend   Yes / No

Experience _____
_____
_____

Date _____

Dispensary (name/location) _____

Strain _____   indica ☐   Price _____ $/g
                                        sativa ☐

Color   ## Crystal   ## Density   ## Scent

Green / Yellow / Orange / Red / Violet (Color wheel)

Large ☐ ☐ Heavy   Rock ☐ Tight   Heavy ☐ ☐ ☐ ☐
Small ☐ ☐ Light   Loose ☐ Airy   Light ☐ ☐ ☐ ☐
Size Coverage   Pine/Earthy Citrus Skunk/Cheese Floral

Description _____

_____

Taste   ## Smoke

Floral / Citrus / Cheese / Nutty / Earthy / Spicy / Peppery / Fruity (Taste wheel)

Heavy ☐ Full
Light ☐ Whispy

Description _____

_____

Overall _____ /10 _____   Recommend   Yes / No

Experience _____

_____

_____

Date _____

Dispensary (name/location) _____

Strain _____

indica ☐
sativa ☐

Price _____ $/

Color

Green Yellow
Blue Orange
Violet Red

Crystal

Large ☐ ☐ Heavy
Small ☐ ☐ Light

Size Coverage

Density

Rock ☐ Tight
Loose ☐ Airy

Scent

Heavy ☐ ☐ ☐ ☐
Light ☐ ☐ ☐

Pine/Earthy Citrus Skunk/Cheese Floral

Description

_____

Taste

Floral Citrus
Fruity Cheese
Peppery Nutty
Spicy Earthy

Smoke

Heavy ☐ Full
Light ☐ Whispy

Description

_____

Overall _____ /10

Recommend Yes / No

Experience

_____

Dispensary (name/location) _____

Strain _____ indica ☐ **Price** _____ $/g
                                          sativa ☐

Color   ### Crystal   ### Density   ### Scent

Color wheel: Green, Yellow, Blue, Orange, Violet, Red

Crystal: Large / Small — Size; Heavy / Light — Coverage

Density: Rock / Loose; Tight / Airy

Scent: Heavy / Light — Pine/Earthy, Citrus, Skunk/Cheese, Floral

Description _____

_____

Taste   ### Smoke

Taste wheel: Floral, Citrus, Cheese, Nutty, Earthy, Spicy, Peppery, Fruity

Smoke: Heavy / Light; Full / Whispy

Description _____

_____

Overall _____ /10 _____   **Recommend** Yes / No

Experience _____

_____

_____

Date _____

Dispensary (name/location) _____

Strain _____ indica ☐ Price _____ $/g
                         sativa ☐

Color

Green Yellow
Blue   Orange
Violet   Red

Crystal

Large ☐ ☐ Heavy
Small ☐ ☐ Light
  Size Coverage

Density

Rock ☐ Tight
Loose ☐ Airy

Scent

Heavy ☐ ☐ ☐ ☐
Light ☐ ☐ ☐ ☐
  Pine/Earthy Citrus Skunk/Cheese Floral

Description

_____
_____

Taste

Floral Citrus
Fruity   Cheese
Peppery   Nutty
  Spicy Earthy

Smoke

Heavy ☐ Full
Light ☐ Whispy

Description

_____
_____

Overall _____ /10 _____   Recommend Yes / No

Experience _____
_____
_____

Date _____

Dispensary (name/location) _____

Strain _____   indica ☐   Price _____ $/g
                          sativa ☐

Color

Green Yellow
              Orange
Violet Red

Crystal

Large ☐ ☐ Heavy
Small ☐ ☐ Light
Size Coverage

Density

Rock ☐ Tight
Loose ☐ Airy

Scent

Heavy ☐ ☐ ☐ ☐
Light
Pine/Earthy Citrus Skunk/Cheese Floral

Description _____

Taste

Floral Citrus
Fruity   Cheese
Peppery   Nutty
  Spicy Earthy

Smoke

Heavy ☐ Full
Light ☐ Whispy

Description
_____
_____

Overall _____ /10 _____   Recommend   Yes / No

Experience
_____
_____
_____

Date _____

Dispensary (name/location) _____

Strain _____   indica ☐   Price _____ $/g
                          sativa ☐

Color

Green Yellow
Blue   Orange
  Violet Red

Crystal

Large ☐ ☐ Heavy
Small ☐ ☐ Light
Size Coverage

Density

Rock ☐ Tight
Loose ☐ Airy

Scent

Heavy ☐ ☐ ☐ ☐
Light
Pine/Earthy Citrus Skunk/Cheese Floral

Description

_____

Taste

Floral Citrus
Fruity   Cheese
Peppery   Nutty
  Spicy Earthy

Smoke

Heavy ☐ Full
Light ☐ Whispy

Description

_____

Overall _____ /10   Recommend Yes / No

Experience

_____
_____

Date _____

Dispensary (name/location) _____

Strain _____   indica ☐   Price _____ $/g
                           sativa ☐

Color

Green — Yellow — Orange — Red — Violet

Crystal

Large ☐ ☐ Heavy
Small ☐ ☐ Light

Size *Coverage*

Density

Rock ☐ Tight
Loose ☐ Airy

Scent

Heavy ☐ ☐ ☐ ☐
Light ☐ ☐ ☐ ☐

Pine/Earthy *Citrus* *Skunk/Cheese* *Floral*

Description _____

Taste

Floral — Citrus — Cheese — Nutty — Earthy — Spicy — Peppery — Fruity

Smoke

Heavy ☐ Full
Light ☐ Whispy

Description _____

Overall _____ /10   Recommend   Yes / No

Experience _____

Date _____

Dispensary (name/location) _____

Strain _____   indica ☐   Price _____ $/
                           sativa ☐

Color

Green Yellow
Blue   Orange
Violet Red

Crystal

Large ☐ ☐ Heavy
Small ☐ ☐ Light

Size   Coverage

Density

Rock ☐ Tight
Loose ☐ Airy

Scent

Heavy ☐ ☐ ☐ ☐
Light ☐ ☐ ☐ ☐

Pine/Earthy   Citrus   Skunk/Cheese   Floral

Description
_____
_____

Taste

Floral Citrus
Fruity   Cheese
Peppery   Nutty
Spicy Earthy

Smoke

Heavy ☐ Full
Light ☐ Whisp.

Description
_____
_____

Overall _____ /10 _____   Recommend   Yes / No

Experience
_____
_____
_____

Date _____

Strain _____ indica ☐ Price _____ $/g
sativa ☐

Color

Green Yellow
Blue   Orange
Violet Red

Crystal

Large ☐ ☐ Heavy
Small ☐ ☐ Light

Size Coverage

Density

Rock ☐ Tight
Loose ☐ Airy

Scent

Heavy ☐ ☐ ☐ ☐
Light

Pine/Earthy Citrus Skunk/Cheese Floral

Description _____

Taste

Floral Citrus
Fruity   Cheese
Peppery   Nutty
Spicy Earthy

Smoke

Heavy ☐ Full
Light ☐ Whispy

Description _____

Overall ____ /10 ____   Recommend Yes / No

Experience _____

Date _____

Dispensary (name/location) _____

Strain _____ indica ☐   Price _____ $/g
  sativa ☐

Color

Green   Yellow
Blue   Orange
Violet   Red

Crystal

Large ▢ ▢ Heavy
Small ▢ ▢ Light
Size   Coverage

Density

Rock ▢ Tight
Loose ▢ Airy

Scent

Heavy ▢ ▢ ▢ ▢
Light ▢ ▢ ▢
Pine/Earthy   Citrus   Skunk/Cheese   Floral

Description _____
_____

Taste

Floral   Citrus
Fruity   Cheese
Peppery   Nutty
Spicy   Earthy

Smoke

Heavy ▢ Full
Light ▢ Whispy

Description _____
_____

Overall _____ /10 _____   Recommend   Yes / No

Experience _____
_____
_____

Date _____

Dispensary (name/location) _____

Strain _____ indica ☐ Price _____ $/g
                                  sativa ☐

Color

Green | Yellow
Violet | Orange
 | Red

Crystal

Large ☐ ☐ Heavy
Small ☐ ☐ Light

Size Coverage

Density

Rock ☐ Tight
Loose ☐ Airy

Scent

Heavy ☐ ☐ ☐ ☐
Light ☐ ☐ ☐ ☐

Pine/Earthy Citrus Skunk/Cheese Floral

Description _____
_____

Taste

Floral Citrus
Fruity   Cheese
Peppery   Nutty
  Spicy Earthy

Smoke

Heavy ☐ Full
Light ☐ Whispy

Description _____
_____

Overall _____ /10 _____   Recommend   Yes / No

Experience _____
_____
_____

Date _____

Dispensary (name/location) _____

Strain _____   indica ☐   Price _____ $/g
                         sativa ☐

Color

Green · Yellow
Blue · Orange
Violet · Red

Crystal

Large ▯ ▯ Heavy
Small ▯ ▯ Light
Size   Coverage

Density

Rock ▯ Tight
Loose ▯ Airy

Scent

Heavy ▯ ▯ ▯ ▯
Light ▯ ▯ ▯ ▯
Pine/Earthy   Citrus   Skunk/Cheese   Floral

Description

_____
_____

Taste

Floral · Citrus
Fruity · Cheese
Peppery · Nutty
Spicy · Earthy

Smoke

Heavy ▯ Full
Light ▯ Whispy

Description

_____
_____

Overall _____ /10 _____   Recommend   Yes / No

Experience

_____
_____
_____

Date _____

Dispensary (name/location) _____

Strain _____   indica ☐   Price _____ $/g
                         sativa ☐

Color   **Crystal**   **Density**   **Scent**

Green Yellow   Large ☐ ☐ Heavy   Rock ☐ Tight   Heavy ☐ ☐ ☐ ☐
       Orange   Light
Small ☐ ☐ Light Loose ☐ Airy
Violet Red   Size Coverage   Pine/Earthy Citrus Skunk/Cheese Floral

Description _____
_____

Taste   **Smoke**

Heavy ☐ Full

Floral Citrus
Fruity   Cheese
                         Light ☐ Whispy
Peppery   Nutty
   Spicy Earthy

Description _____
_____

Overall _____ /10 _____   Recommend   Yes / No

Experience _____
_____
_____

Date _____

Dispensary (name/location) _____

Strain _____   indica ☐   Price _____ $/
                          sativa ☐

Color
Green Yellow
Blue   Orange
  Violet   Red

Crystal
Large ☐ ☐ Heavy
Small ☐ ☐ Light
      Size Coverage

Density
Rock ☐ Tight
Loose ☐ Airy

Scent
Heavy ☐ ☐ ☐ ☐
Light ☐ ☐ ☐ ☐
Pine/Earthy Citrus Skunk/Cheese Floral

Description
_____
_____

Taste
Floral Citrus
Fruity   Cheese
Peppery   Nutty
  Spicy Earthy

Smoke
Heavy ☐ Full
Light ☐ Whispy

Description
_____
_____

Overall _____ /10 _____   Recommend   Yes / No

Experience
_____
_____
_____

Date _____

Dispensary (name/location) _____

Strain _____ indica ☐ Price _____ $/g
                          sativa ☐

Color

Green Yellow
Blue   Orange
Violet Red

Crystal

Large ☐ ☐ Heavy
Small ☐ ☐ Light
Size Coverage

Density

Rock ☐ Tight
Loose ☐ Airy

Scent

Heavy ☐ ☐ ☐ ☐
Light
Pine/Earthy Citrus Skunk/Cheese Floral

Description _____

Taste

Floral Citrus
Fruity   Cheese
Peppery   Nutty
  Spicy Earthy

Smoke

Heavy ☐ Full
Light ☐ Whispy

Description _____

Overall _____ /10 _____   Recommend   Yes / No

Experience _____

Date _____

Dispensary (name/location) _____

Strain _____   indica ☐   Price _____ $/g
                          sativa ☐

Color
Green / Yellow
Blue / Orange
Violet / Red

Crystal
Large ☐ ☐ Heavy
Small ☐ ☐ Light
Size Coverage

Density
Rock ☐ Tight
Loose ☐ Airy

Scent
Heavy ☐ ☐ ☐ ☐
Light ☐ ☐ ☐ ☐
Pine/Earthy Citrus Skunk/Cheese Floral

Description _____
_____

Taste
Floral Citrus
Fruity   Cheese
Peppery   Nutty
Spicy Earthy

Smoke
Heavy ☐ Full
Light ☐ Whispy

Description _____
_____

Overall _____ /10 _____   Recommend   Yes / No

Experience _____
_____
_____

Date _____

Dispensary (name/location) _____

Strain _____ indica ☐ Price _____ $/g
                             sativa ☐

Color   ## Crystal   ## Density   ## Scent

Green Yellow
Blue Orange
Violet Red

Large ☐ ☐ Heavy
Small ☐ ☐ Light
Size *Coverage*

Rock ☐ Tight
Loose ☐ Airy

Heavy ☐ ☐ ☐ ☐
Light
Pine/Earthy *Citrus* *Skunk/Cheese* *Floral*

Description _____

Taste   ## Smoke

Floral Citrus
Fruity Cheese
Peppery Nutty
Spicy Earthy

Heavy ☐ Full
Light ☐ Whispy

Description _____
_____

Overall _____ /10   Recommend   Yes / No

Experience _____
_____

Date _____

Dispensary (name/location) _____

Strain _____ indica ☐ Price _____ $/g
                         sativa ☐

Color

Green Yellow
Blue   Orange
Violet Red

Crystal

Large ☐ ☐ Heavy
Small ☐ ☐ Light

Size Coverage

Density

Rock ☐ Tight
Loose ☐ Airy

Scent

Heavy ☐ ☐ ☐ ☐
Light ☐ ☐ ☐ ☐

Pine/Earthy Citrus Skunk/Cheese Floral

Description _____

_____

Taste

Floral Citrus
Fruity   Cheese
Peppery   Nutty
Spicy Earthy

Smoke

Heavy ☐ Full
Light ☐ Whispy

Description _____

_____

Overall _____ /10

Recommend Yes / No

Experience _____

_____

_____

Dispensary (name/location) _____

Strain _____   indica ☐   Price _____ $/g
                                     sativa ☐

Color   ## Crystal   ## Density   ## Scent

Green Yellow   Large ☐ ☐ Heavy   Rock ☐ Tight   Heavy ☐ ☐ ☐ ☐
                 Small ☐ ☐ Light   Loose ☐ Airy   Light ☐ ☐ ☐ ☐
       Orange
                      Size Coverage   Pine/Earthy Citrus Skunk/Cheese Floral
Violet Red

Description _____

Taste   ## Smoke

Floral Citrus   Heavy ☐ Full
Fruity   Cheese
Peppery   Nutty   Light ☐ Whispy
   Spicy Earthy

Description _____
_____

Overall _____ /10 _____   Recommend   Yes / No

Experience _____
_____
_____

Date _____

Dispensary (name/location) _____

Strain _____

indica ☐
sativa ☐

Price _____ $/

Color

Green Yellow
Blue Orange
Violet Red

Crystal

Large ☐ ☐ Heavy
Small ☐ ☐ Light

Size Coverage

Density

Rock ☐ Tight
Loose ☐ Airy

Scent

Heavy ☐ ☐ ☐ ☐ Light

Pine/Earthy Citrus Skunk/Cheese Floral

Description _____

_____

Taste

Floral Citrus
Fruity Cheese
Peppery Nutty
Spicy Earthy

Smoke

Heavy ☐ Full
Light ☐ Whispy

Description _____

_____

Overall _____ /10

Recommend   Yes / No

Experience _____

_____

_____

Date _____

Dispensary (name/location) _____

Strain _____ indica ☐ Price _____ $/g
                                   sativa ☐

Color

Green Yellow
Blue   Orange
  Violet   Red

Crystal

Large ☐ ☐ Heavy

Small ☐ ☐ Light

Size *Coverage*

Density

Rock ☐ Tight

Loose ☐ Airy

Scent

Heavy ☐ ☐ ☐ ☐
Light ☐ ☐ ☐ ☐

Pine/Earthy *Citrus* *Skunk/Cheese* *Floral*

Description _____

Taste

Floral Citrus
Fruity   Cheese
Peppery   Nutty
  Spicy   Earthy

Smoke

Heavy ☐ Full

Light ☐ Whispy

Description _____
_____

Overall _____ /10 _____   Recommend   Yes / No

Experience _____
_____

I hope you enjoyed "working" your way through this journal.

May this be an addition to many volumes of

The Chronnoisseur

in your collection!

www.ingramcontent.com/pod-product-compliance
Lightning Source LLC
Chambersburg PA
CBHW050352290526
45785CB00006B/2740